Mushroom Coloring Book For Adults

30 Hand Drawn, Woodland And Nature Themed Mushrom And Toadstool Adult Coloring Pages

By
Louise Ford

ISBN-13: 978-1540412225
ISBN-10: 1540412229

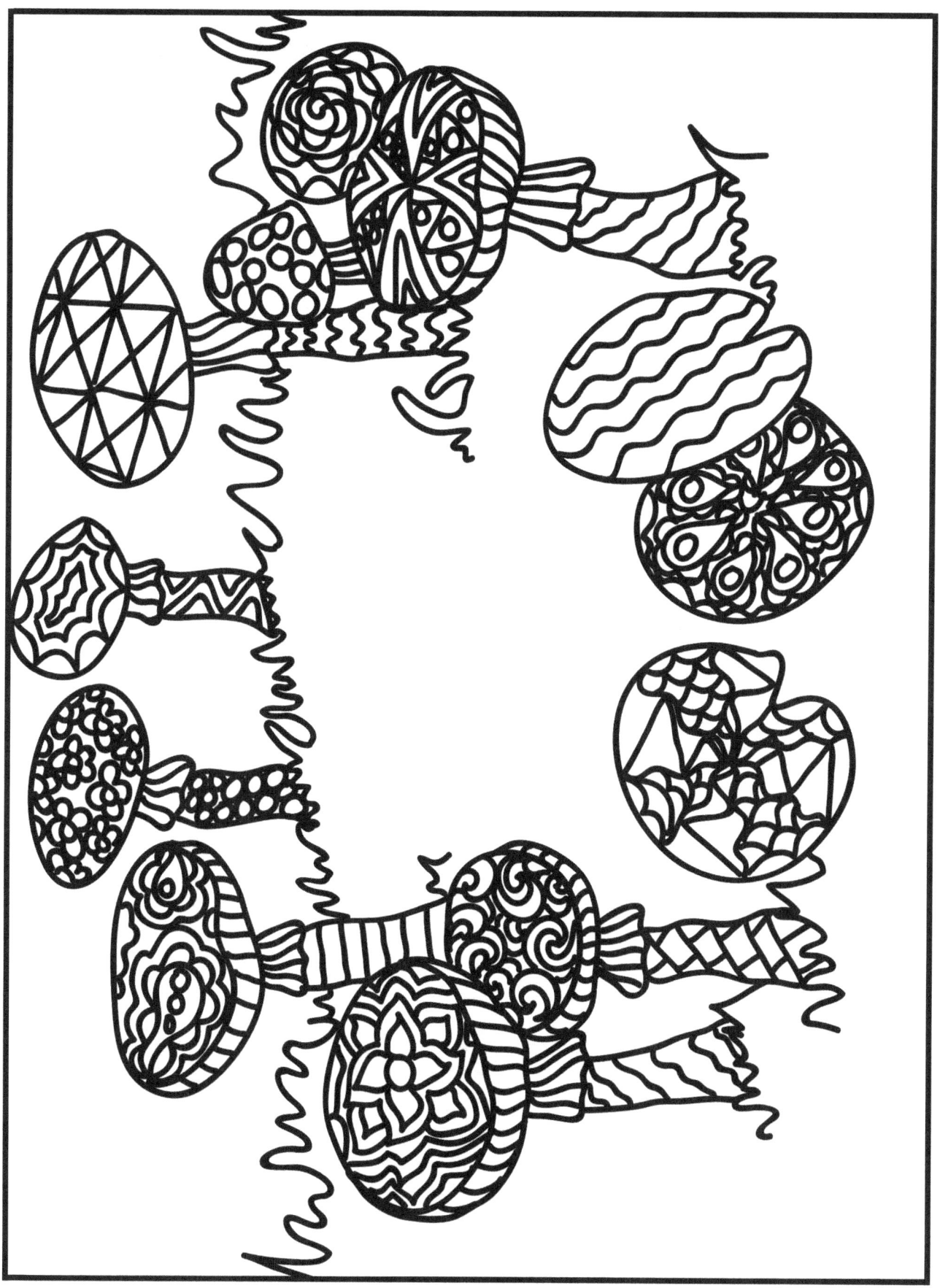

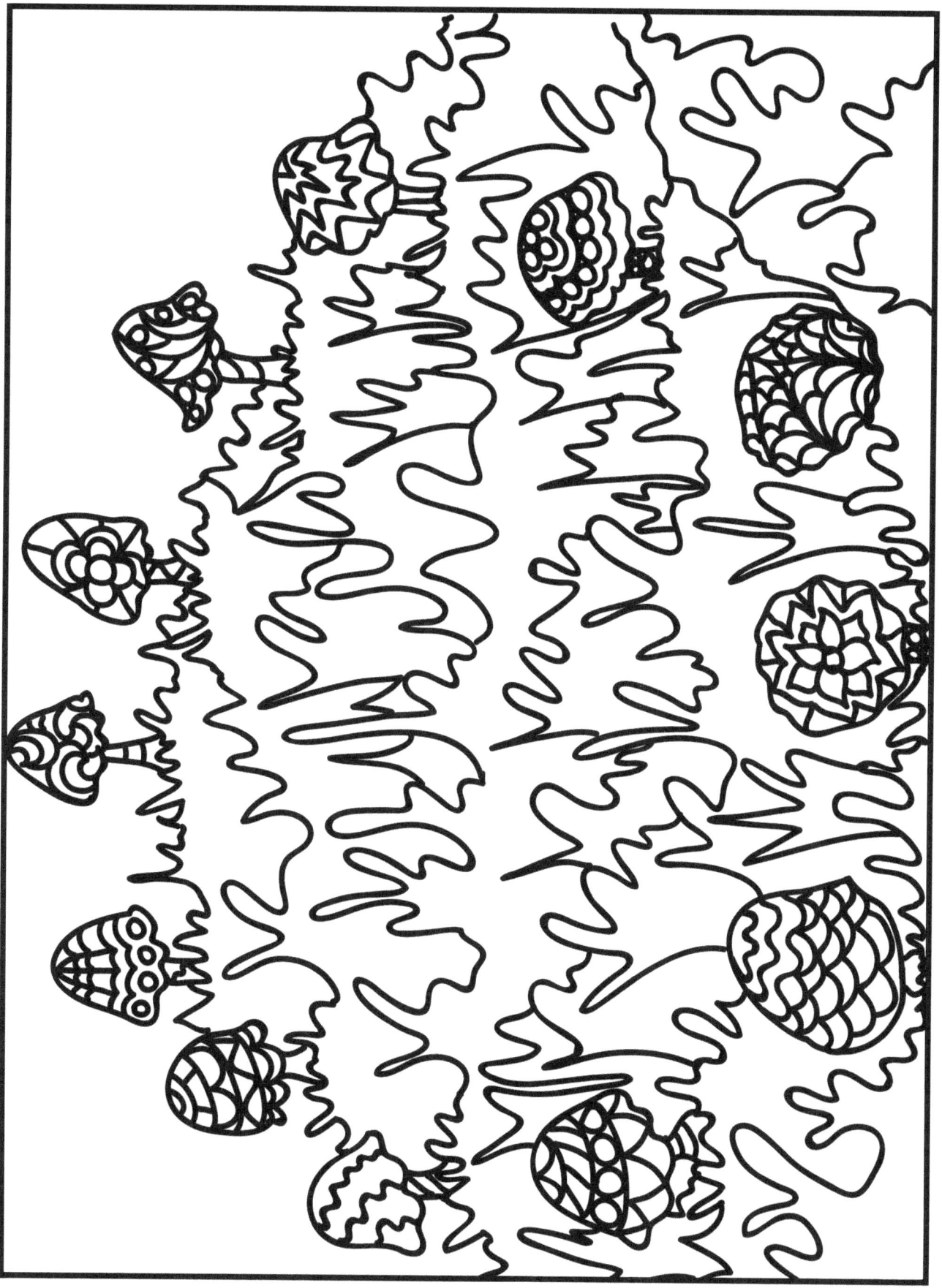

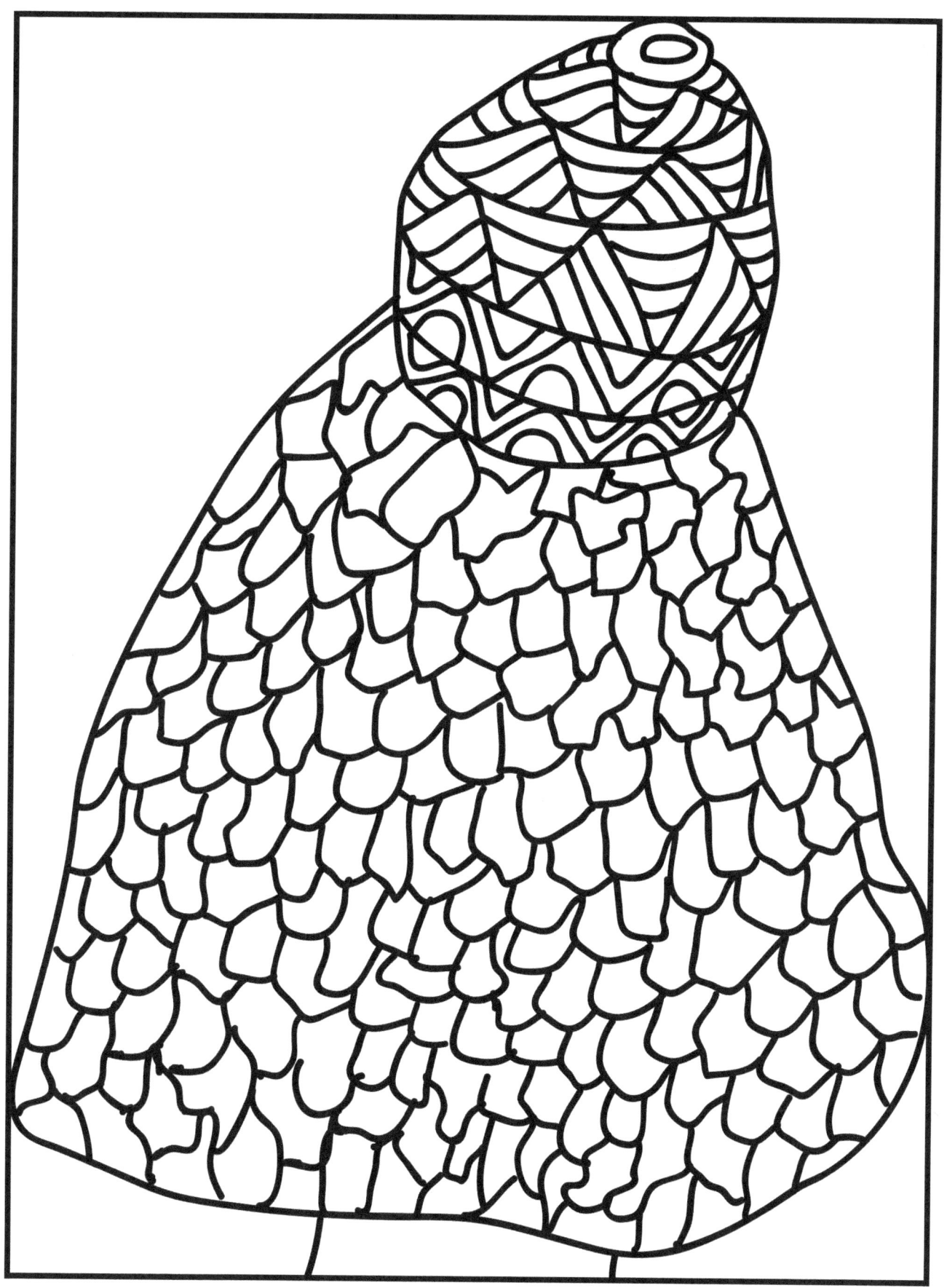

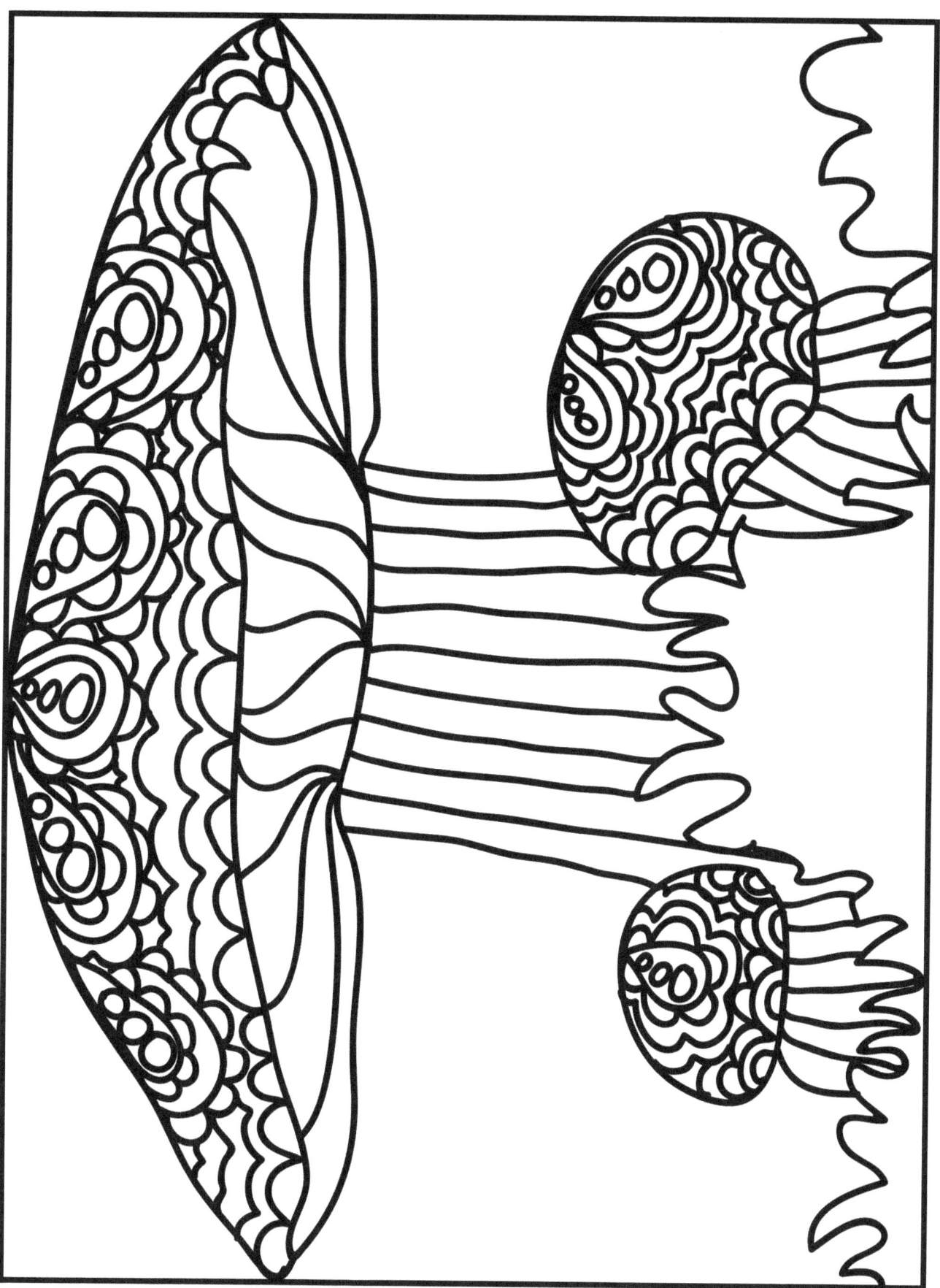

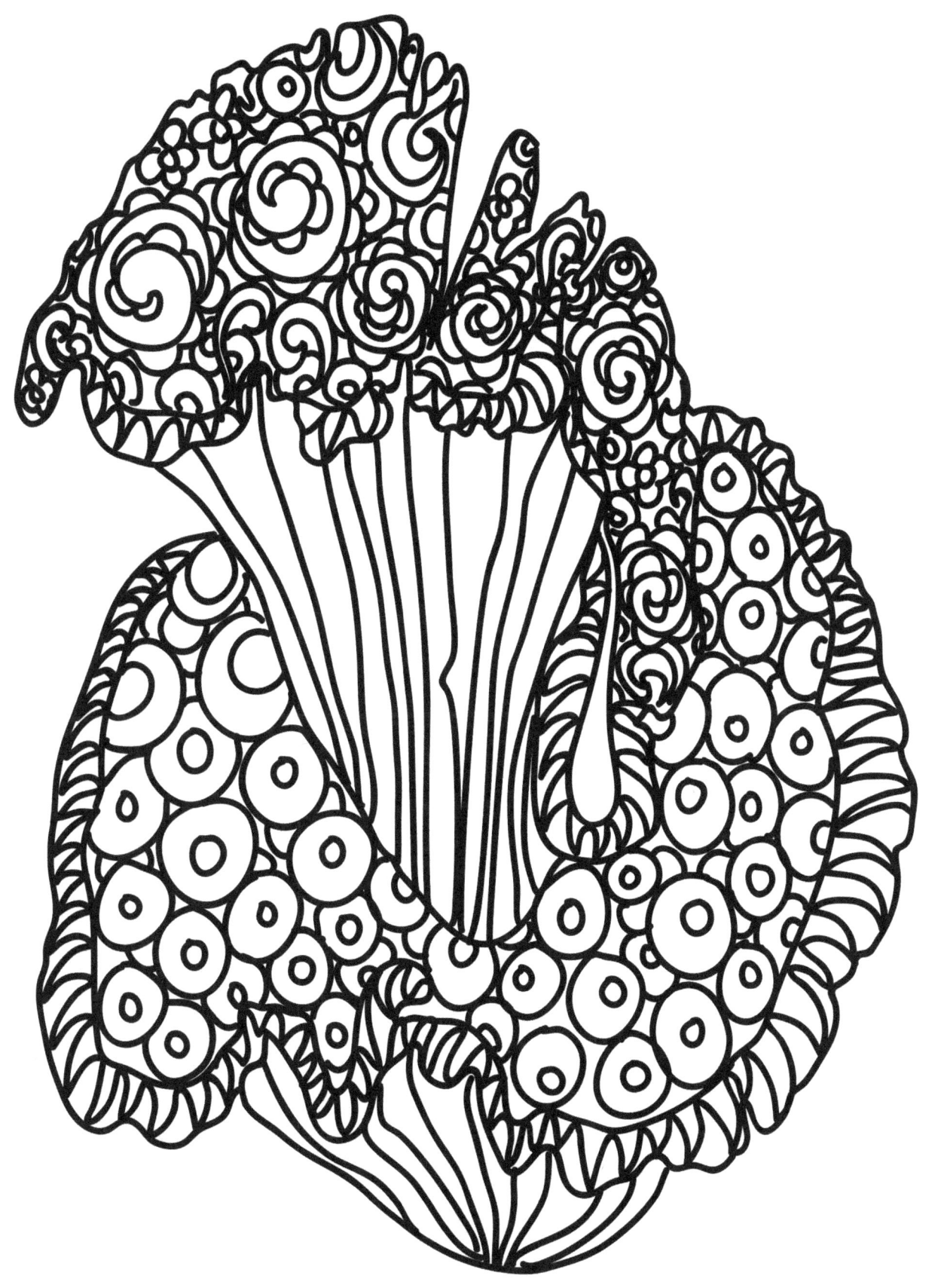

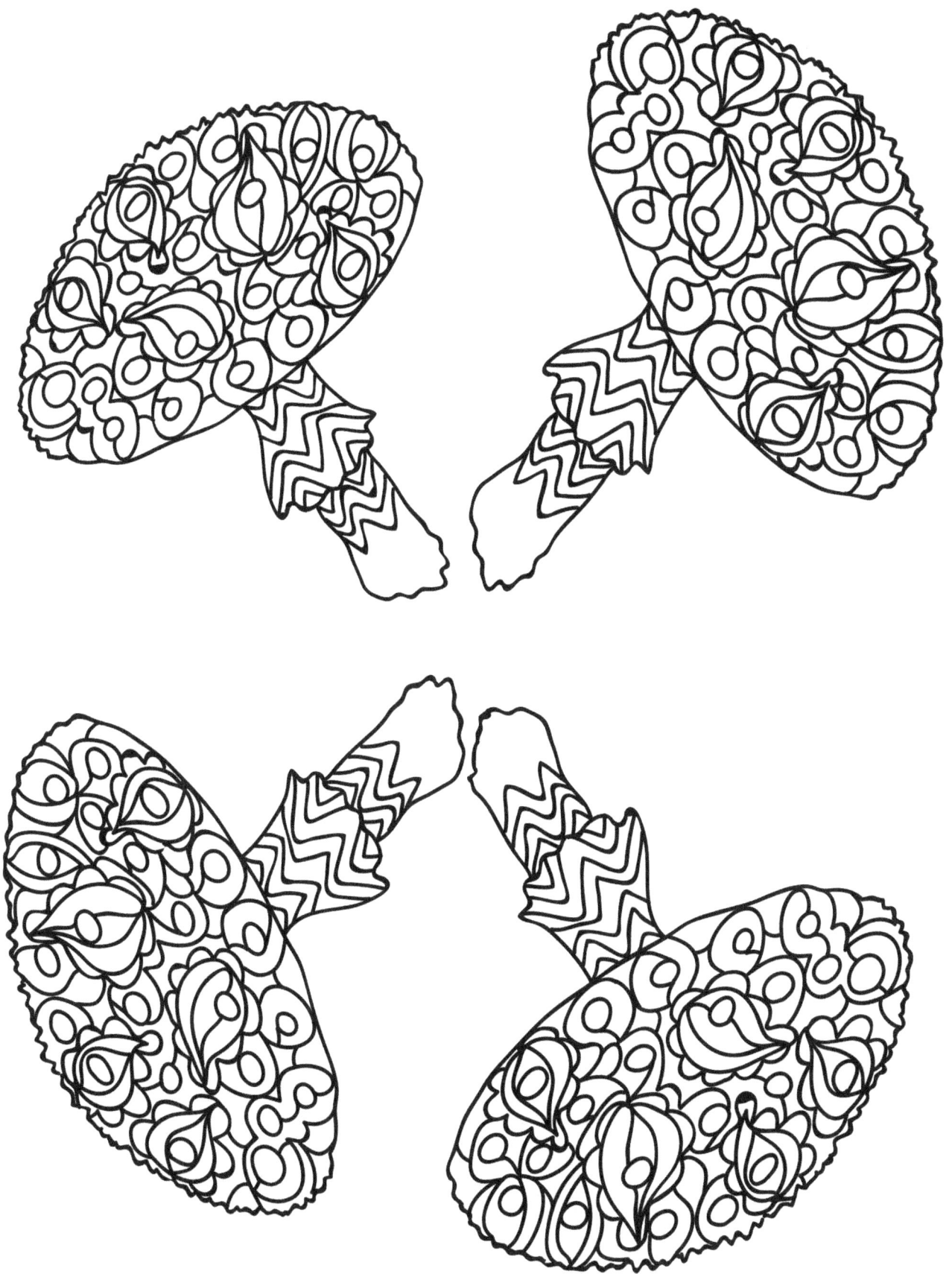

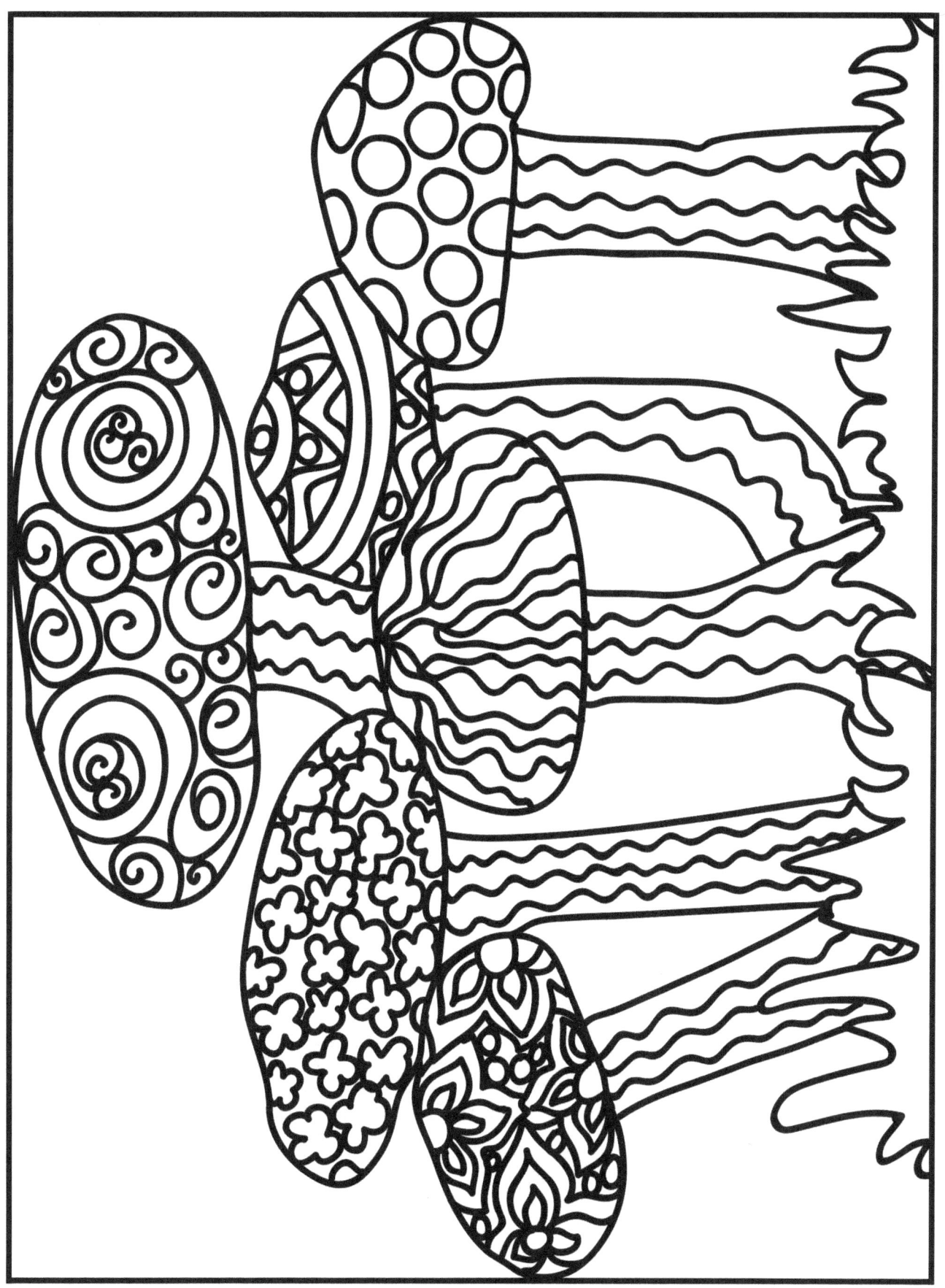

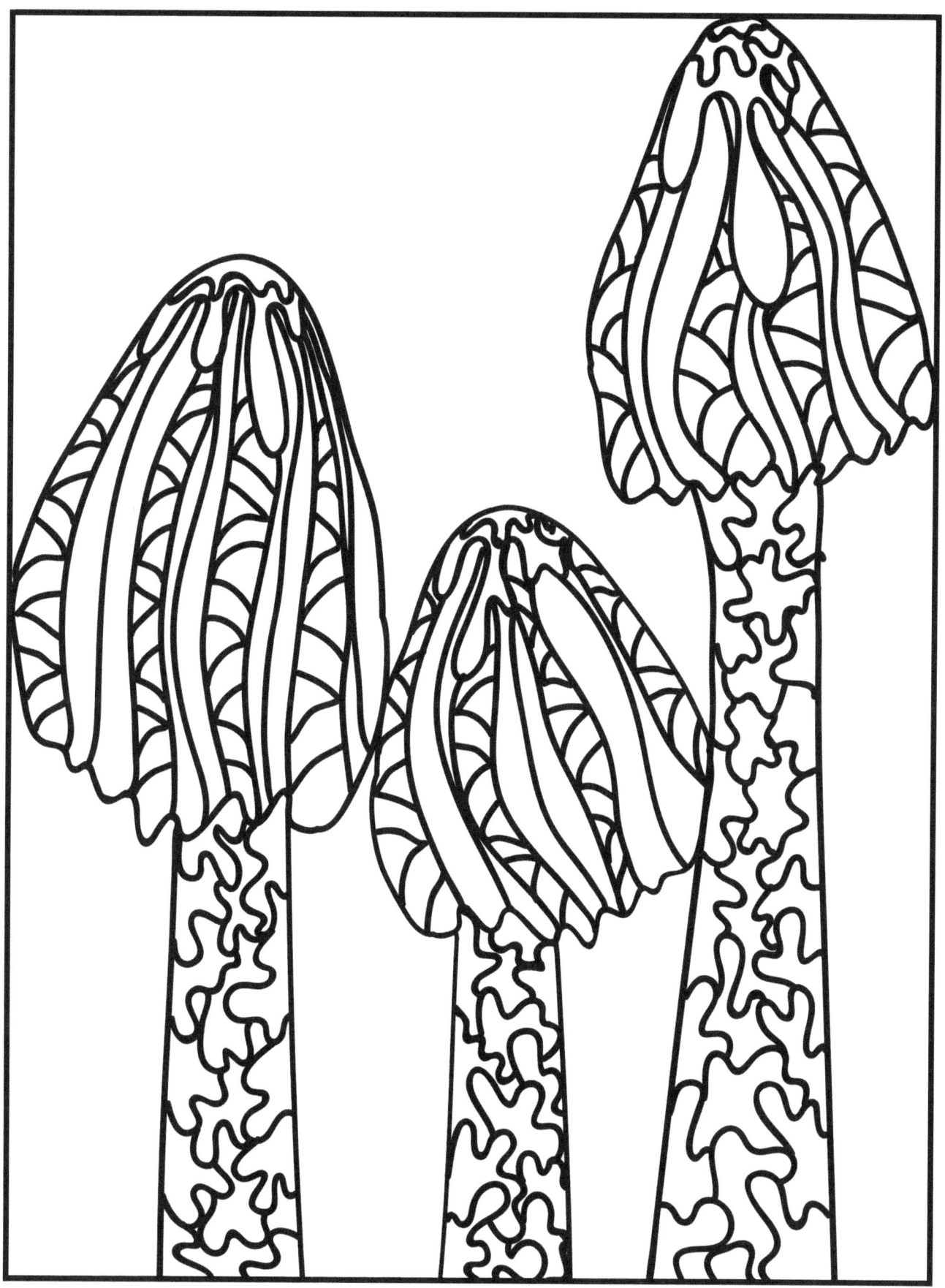

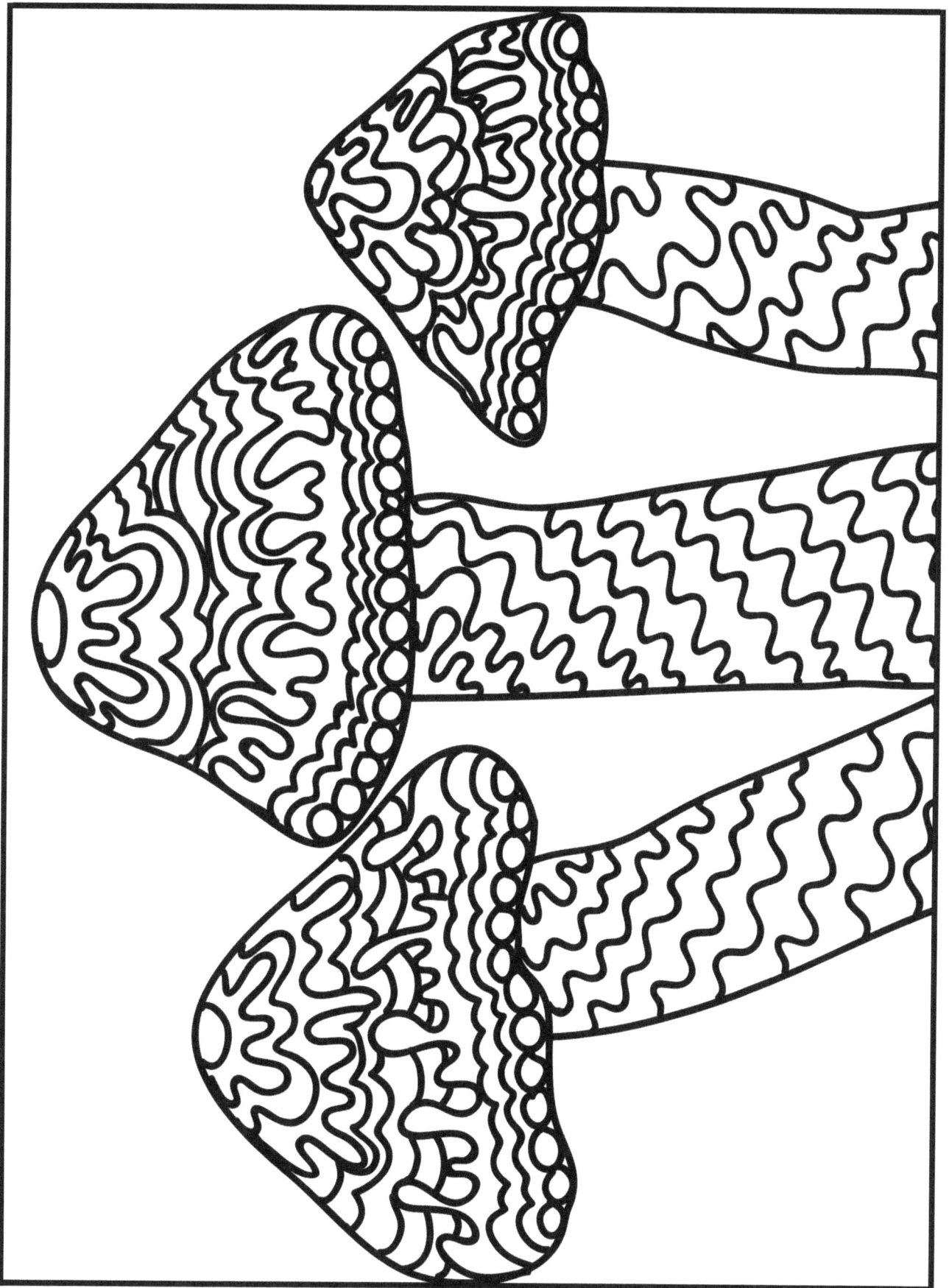

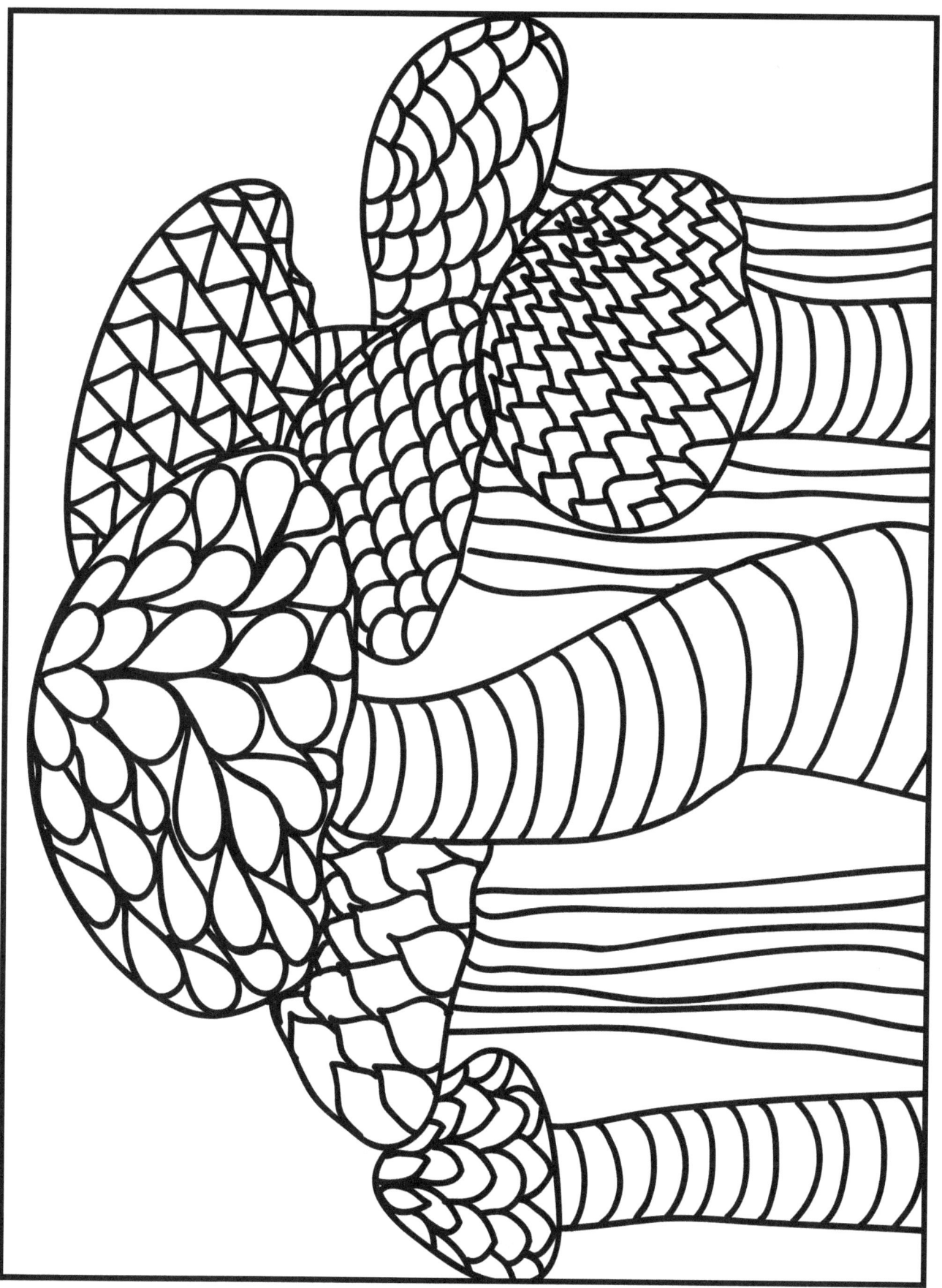

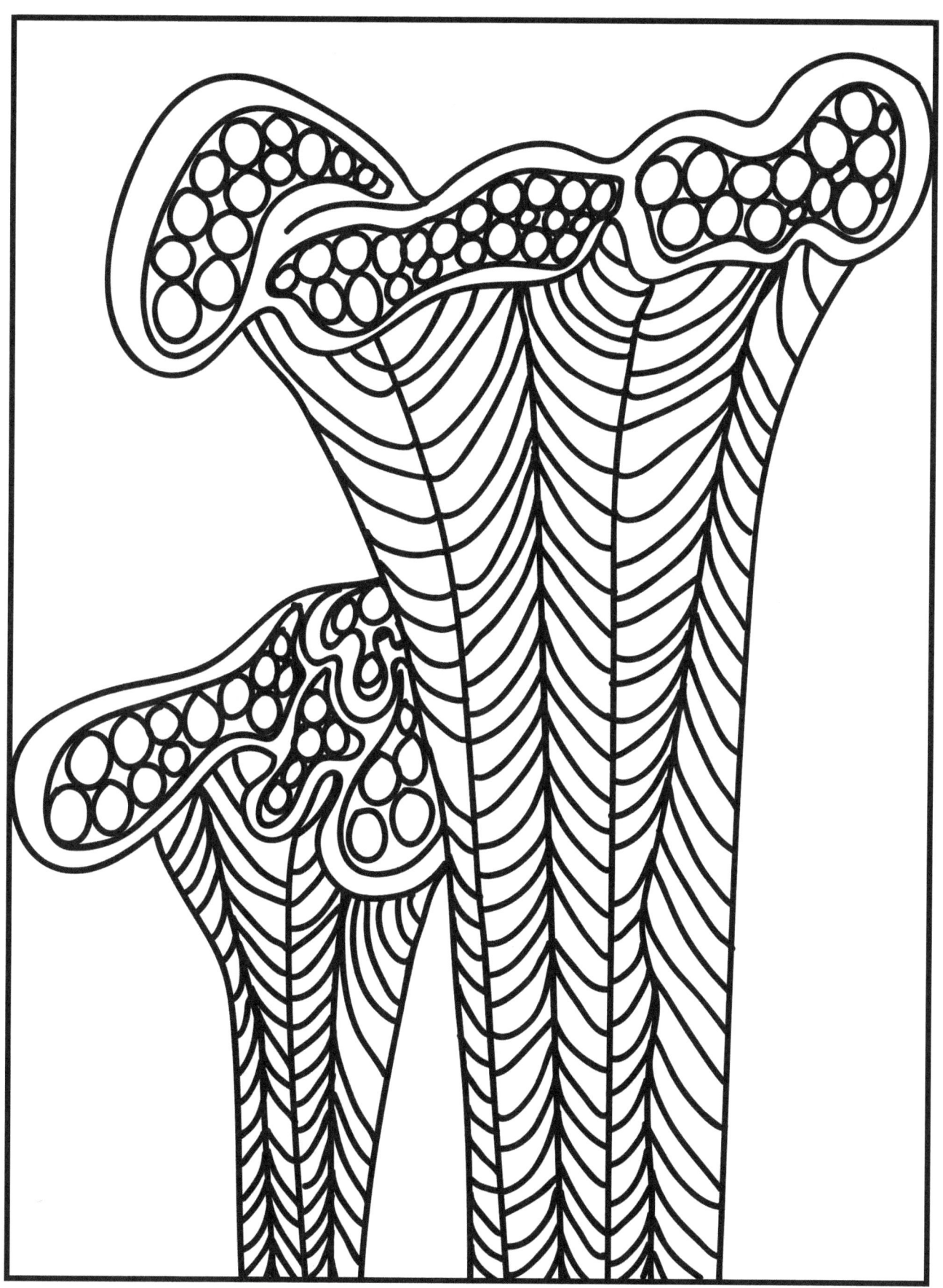

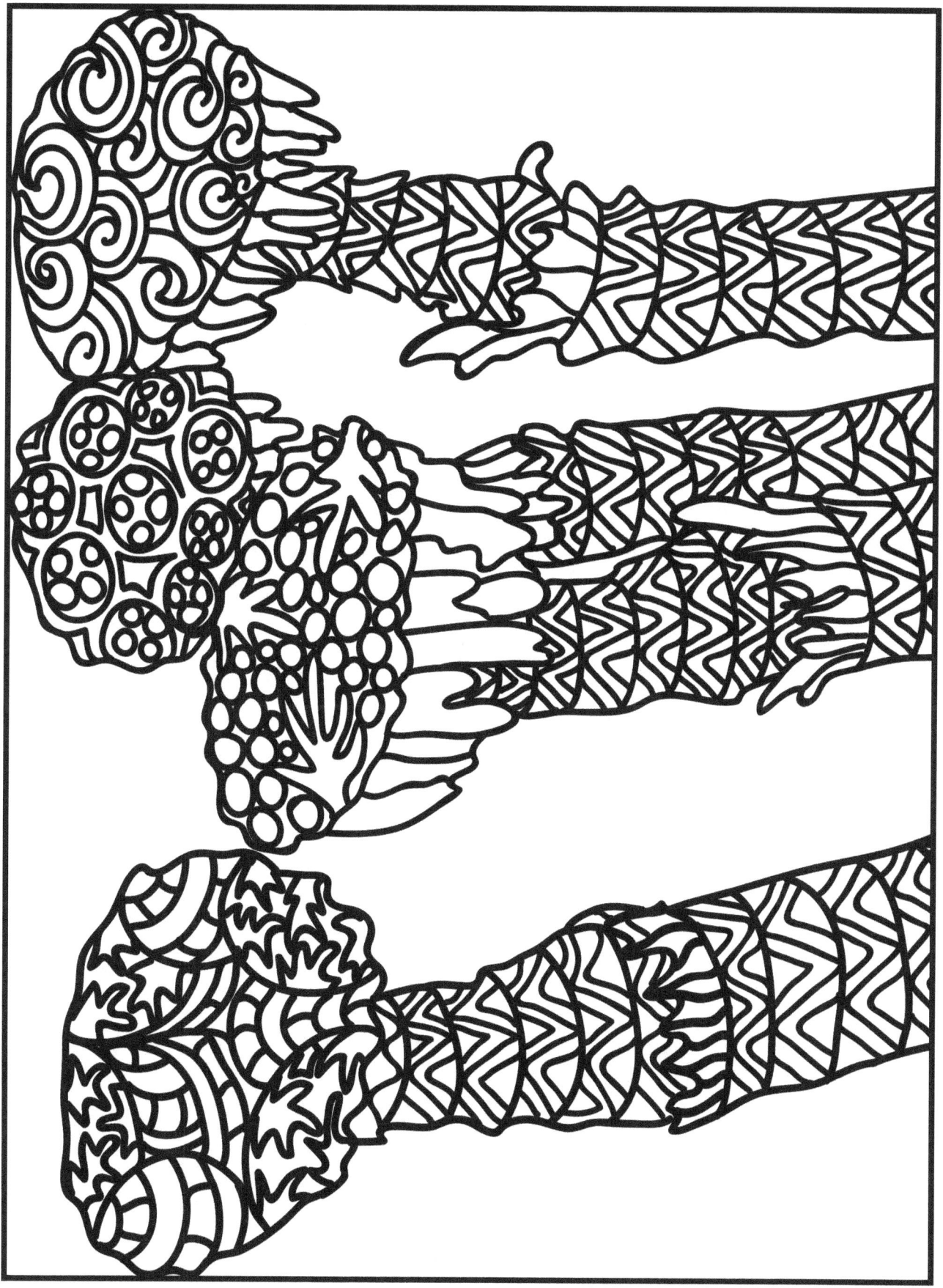

www.ingramcontent.com/pod-product-compliance
Lightning Source LLC
Chambersburg PA
CBHW081859280526
45789CB00007B/2762